# BROKE NO MORE

## A Money Blueprint for Young Ambition and Financial Resilience

## Terence Correl

# Introduction

Are you a young adult who's feeling a bit adrift when it comes to managing your finances? You're not alone. Many young people lack the vital skill of financial literacy, and navigating the intricacies of money can be quite the challenge without proper guidance. Numerous individuals have faced setbacks due to their lack of financial know-how, leaving them struggling to thrive.

Introducing "Broke No More: A Money Blueprint for Young Ambition and Financial Resilience." This book is all about providing you with pragmatic advice and direction, empowering you to seize control of your finances and establish a sturdy economic groundwork for your future.

But why is financial literacy so crucial? Let's be honest – money is a universal constant. Whether it's grappling with student loans, striving to save for a home down payment, or merely making ends meet, money shapes our lives significantly. Without a strong grasp of effective financial management, you could find yourself in a precarious position, something you might have already experienced as a young individual.

Enter this book. It delves into a comprehensive array of personal finance topics, spanning from budgeting and debt management to investment strategies and wealth accumulation. Real-life illustrations are woven throughout the book to elucidate the discussed concepts, and actionable insights are generously provided to help you put these ideas into concrete practice.

By the book's conclusion, you'll possess a firm comprehension of personal finance intricacies and wield the necessary tools for triumph. Crafting a budget tailored to your lifestyle, adeptly managing your debts, planning for the future, and gradually amassing wealth will all be within your grasp. If you're ready to steer your financial journey, this book is your ideal companion. Let's embark on this transformative path together!

# Chapter One

## Money Mindset

Welcome to "Broke No More: A Money Blueprint for Young Ambition and Financial Resilience"! In the pages ahead, we'll explore how to navigate your finances and achieve financial freedom, even if you're starting from scratch or working hard to make ends meet. But before we delve into the details of money management, let's talk about something equally important: your mindset.

## The Importance of a Positive Money Mindset

Your mindset can have a profound impact on your financial success. If you believe that money is scarce and hard to come by, you're likely to struggle with money management and feel stressed about your finances. On the other hand, if you have a positive money mindset and believe that money is abundant and within your reach, you're more likely to attract wealth and opportunities. This is referred to as the law of attraction. What you believe or the state of your mindset becomes your reality. What you believe, you attract.

But what exactly is a positive money mindset? It's a way of thinking that focuses on abundance, possibility, and growth, rather than scarcity, fear, and lack. It's about believing that you can create wealth and live the life you want, even if you don't have much money right now. It's also about being mindful of your thoughts and emotions around money and reframing any negative beliefs or attitudes.

All these are mind-conditioning for money attraction. When you condition your mind for positivity, it doesn't just redefine your mindset about money or wealth creation; it extends to every aspect of your life, from relationship, to quality networks, to career and opportunities, to health. Let me tell you a quick story.

I used to believe that money was scarce and hard to come by, which led to a lot of stress and anxiety around my finances. This belief affected the way I saw money. And believe, money was very hard to come my way. I would work so hard, but I was getting little to nothing to survive. And I often wondered why. But when I started shifting my mindset towards abundance, everything changed.

My work input was now in synchronization with my mind output. My eyes were opened. And I could see that I had been limiting the flow of money into my life by my thought patterns. I realized that money responds to what you think. I often thought I don't deserve so much money. Therefore, my mind conditioning limited the flow of money into my life.

Instead of worrying about what I didn't have, I focused on what I did have and started feeling grateful for it. I started a gratitude journal where I wrote down three things, I was thankful for every day. It could be something as simple as having a warm bed to sleep in or a good meal to eat. This helped me shift my focus from scarcity to abundance.

Looking back now, I'm grateful I was able to recondition my mindset on money. So, let's see how you can recondition your mindset just as I was able to.

## How To Shift Your Mindset Towards Abundance and Away from Scarcity:

Shifting your mindset towards abundance is not always easy, especially if you've grown up with limited resources or experienced financial hardship. But it's a skill that can be learned and practiced, and the rewards are worth it.

*Here are some tips to help you shift your mindset towards abundance:*

- **Gratitude:** Cultivate a sense of gratitude for what you have, rather than focusing on what you lack. This is the power in shifting your thought pattern from lack to abundance. Take time every day to appreciate the good things in your life, whether it's a roof over your head, a meal on the table, or a supportive friend.

  Another thing that has helped me is practicing generosity. Even when I didn't have a lot of money, I found that giving what I could to others helped me feel more abundant. It could be something as simple as buying a coffee for a friend or volunteering at a local charity.

  The activity of gratitude and generosity helps you to stay focused on abundance mindset. It then sinks to your subconscious such that it becomes part of your reality.

- **Visualization:** Visualize yourself achieving your financial goals and living the life you want. Create a vision board or write down your goals and dreams, and imagine yourself already there. This can help you stay motivated and focused on what you want, rather than what you don't want.

  When I started working on shifting my mindset, I had to set up a vision board in my bedroom with pictures of the things

I wanted to achieve, like traveling the world and buying a home.

When I wake up in the morning, it was one of the first things I set my eyes on. Before I turned off the light to sleep, it was one of the last things my eyes rested on. Seeing those images every day helped me stay focused on my goals and believe that they were possible. It reminded me of where I wanted to be.

- **Affirmations:** Use positive affirmations to reinforce your beliefs about money and abundance. Repeat phrases like "I am abundant," "Money flows easily and effortlessly to me," or "I am worthy of wealth and success." This can help you rewire your brain and overcome any negative self-talk.

From my story, you will guess correctly I used to struggle with feeling like I wasn't worthy of wealth and success. I tried affirmations as part of mind-shifting journey. Repeating affirmations like "I am worthy of abundance" and "Money flows easily and effortlessly to me" helped me rewire my thinking.

Personally, when I ask young people why they don't use affirmations, they give me the look of someone who feels something is too *old-school* to give it a try. If you're young and you're reading this book, I implore you to practise affirmations, not just relating to your financial life, but to other aspects of your life. There's power in what you say to yourself.

- **Education:** Learn more about money management, investing, and wealth creation. Knowledge is power, and the more you know, the more confident you'll feel about your ability to build wealth and manage your finances.

I used to be intimidated by investing and financial planning. This was before my mindshift journey. I thought investing and finance planning was something very scary. Immediately I took up reading books and articles on personal finances, I gained so much clarity. It was as if the scales of ignorance cleared from my eyes.

I didn't stopped there. I went as far as getting courses on investing and finance management, taking every opportunity to gain knowledge on how money works. I became much confident. Looking back as I write this book, I feel very fulfilled knowing I am well-grounded when it comes to money.

You should take the step to educate yourself more on money and finances as a young individual. Getting this book is just one step of the many steps you will take to get to where you desire. And it never stops. I keep on getting educated every day so I can stay top of my money game.

- **Community:** Surround yourself with people who share your goals and values. Join a financial support group, attend workshops or seminars, or connect with like-minded individuals online. Having a community of support can help you stay motivated and accountable, and provide valuable resources and advice.

Finally, surrounding myself with like-minded people has been invaluable and it still till today. I used to feel like I was the only one struggling with money, but connecting with others who were on a similar journey helped me feel less alone. I joined a financial support group and attended workshops and seminars, which gave me access to resources and advice that I wouldn't have found on my own.

Also, if possible if your circle consists of individuals who are negative-willed, maybe you should consider finding a new circle. In a circle of five smart individual, when you join them, you become the sixth smart one. As you want to take the journey to shift your money mindset as a young man or woman, maybe you should consider leaving those behind who aren't willing to do the same. It's all about personal choices.

Finally, shifting your mindset towards abundance is a journey, not a destination. Be patient with yourself, and practice these tips consistently over time. With a positive money mindset, you can achieve financial freedom and live the life you want. I guarantee you this.

# Chapter Two

## Budgeting Basics

If you're a young individual and are broke, one of the most important things you can do for your financial future is to create a budget. But what does budgeting mean?

*Budgeting is the process of creating a plan for how to allocate and manage your financial resources over a given period of time, usually on a monthly or annual basis. It involves looking at your income (what you earn), expenses (what you spend money on), and financial goals, and making decisions about how much money to spend, save, or invest in each area of your life.*

For example, imagine you are a working adult who earns a salary and has monthly expenses such as rent, groceries, utilities, transportation, and entertainment. You may create a budget to help you manage your money effectively and achieve your financial goals.

To start, you would need to calculate your total monthly income, which may include your salary, any bonuses, or other sources of income. Then, you would list out all of your monthly expenses and estimate how much you typically spend in each category. This may involve looking at past bank statements or receipts to get an accurate picture of your spending habits.

Once you have a clear understanding of your income and expenses, you can begin to make decisions about how to allocate your money. You may decide to set aside a certain amount each month for savings or investments, while also budgeting for your essential expenses and any discretionary spending.

Throughout the month, you would track your spending and adjust your budget as needed to stay on track and ensure you are not overspending. This may involve making difficult decisions about cutting back on non-essential expenses in order to stay within your budget.

Overall, you can see that budgeting is an important tool for managing your money effectively and achieving your financial goals. By taking a proactive approach to your finances and making intentional decisions about how to allocate your resources, you can improve your financial well-being and reduce stress around money.

That explained, why is budgeting important to you as a young individual?

## The Importance of Budgeting

Budgeting is important because it allows you to take control of your money. I learned this the hard way in my early twenties when I landed my first job after college. I was young and had no idea why budgeting was important. I had the belief that when money comes, you use it to sort things out immediately.

I was making a decent salary, but I had no idea how to manage my money. I would spend my entire paycheck within a few days of getting it and then struggle to make ends meet for the rest of the month. After my personal desire to learn about money, I got to know why budgeting was important. I started putting it to practice, and thus was able to get finances under control. Today, I earn so much from investments, my jobs, and businesses, yet I always make it a point of call to make both monthly and yearly budgets.

When you create a budget, you're making a plan for how you're going to spend your money. This means you can prioritize your expenses, make sure your bills get paid on time, and avoid overspending. For example, my friend Sarah is a freelance writer, and she relies on her budget to make sure she can pay her bills and still have money left over to pursue her passions. She was one of the first persons who inspired me to practice budgeting. As a young individual, this is what budgeting can help you do, so you don't do freebies with your hard-earned money.

Budgeting also helps you track your spending and identify areas where you can cut back. When you see where your money is going, you can make adjustments to your spending habits and save more money for your financial goals. For instance, my brother Matt used to spend a lot of money on takeout food. But after he started tracking his spending, he realized how much he was spending on food each month and decided to start cooking more at home.

Let's move on to creating a budget that works for you.

## How To Create a Budget That Works for You

Creating a budget that works for you starts with understanding your income and expenses. When you have these firmly mapped out, it becomes easy. To begin, start by making a list of all your sources of income, including your salary, any side hustles, and any other money you receive each month.

For example, there was a time I had to go into freelancing; I would create a new budget every month based on the amount of money I expected to earn. I made a projection based on what I made from the previous month. For instance, if I made $3000 the previous month, my projection for the next month would be based on everything that summed up to give me $3000 previously.

Next, make a list of all your monthly expenses, including rent or mortgage payments, utilities, groceries, transportation, and any other bills you have to pay. Don't forget to include expenses like entertainment and dining out – these may seem small, but they can add up quickly! When making my budget back then, I also factor miscellaneous expenses like concerts, dinner outings with friends, charity and support, and personal fun time into the budget.

Once you have a list of your income and expenses, you can create a budget. Start by subtracting your expenses from your income. If you have money left over, that's great – you can use it to save for your financial goals. If your expenses are more than your income, you'll need to find ways to cut back or increase your income. My friend Joe who belonged to the same community while I was learning about money, for example, started driving for a rideshare company to supplement his income when his expenses started to outweigh his income. Personally, I also had to take up other side hustles, when I wanted to step up my earnings.

Following the above simple steps, you can make a decent budget that would work for you based on your earnings. Also, it's one thing to create a budget; it's another thing to stick to them. Let me show you how you can go about it.

## Tips for Sticking to Your Budget

Creating a budget is one thing, but sticking to it can be a challenge. Here are some tips to help you stay on track:

- **Be Realistic:** When you're creating your budget, be realistic about your expenses. Don't underestimate how much you'll spend on things like groceries or transportation – it's better to overestimate and have money left over than to underestimate and run out of money. I made this mistake early on, and found myself constantly dipping into my savings. My saving grace was when I had to retrospect and come to terms with what was truly my expenses.

- **Track Your Spending:** Keep track of your spending throughout the month to make sure you're sticking to your budget. There are plenty of budgeting apps and tools that can help you do this. There are many apps available for tracking your spending, some of which are:

  **Mint:** This is a free app that helps you create a budget, track your spending, and monitor your credit score.

  **PocketGuard:** This app allows you to track your spending and provides alerts when you are nearing your budget limits.

  **YNAB (You Need a Budget):** This app helps you create a budget and stick to it by tracking your expenses and providing feedback.

  **Personal Capital:** This app provides a comprehensive view of your finances, including investments and retirement accounts, as well as budget tracking.

  **Clarity Money:** This app provides budget tracking, expense categorization, and alerts for subscriptions and recurring payments.

**Wally:** This app helps you track your spending and set financial goals by categorizing your expenses and providing insights into your spending habits.

**Honeydue:** This app is designed for couples to track their joint expenses and share information about bills and budgets.

**Expensify:** This app is designed for business use and allows you to track expenses and receipts for reimbursement purposes.

These are just a few examples of the many apps available for tracking your spending. It's important to find the one that best fits your needs and preferences.

- **Find Ways To Save:** Look for ways to cut back on your expenses, like cooking at home instead of eating out or taking public transportation instead of driving. It is up to you on how well you can succeed with this. If you are willing to sacrifice some luxury so you can enjoy comfort later, then you've successfully gotten the hack to cultivate a savings' culture.

- **Make It Fun:** Budgeting doesn't have to be boring! Make it fun by setting goals for yourself and rewarding yourself when you meet them. You could decide to treat yourself to a spa or massage when you meet your goals.

As a young man or woman trying to find his or her feet, and having a grasp of personal finance management, budgeting is an important aspect of the journey that will help you achieve your financial goals. With a little bit of effort, dedication, and commitment, you can create a budget that works for you and stick to it. I did it and succeeded, and so can you.

# Chapter Three

## Debt Management Strategies

Debt is scary. Yet, it is something that intertwines the lives of most young individuals around the globe. Here are some statistics to substantiate the reality of things on ground.

***Based On Types Of Debts:*** According to a 2021 report by the Federal Reserve Bank of New York, the most common types of debt held by young Americans (ages 18-29) are student loans (44%), followed by credit card debt (38%), car loans (21%), and mortgages (4%).

A 2019 report by Eurostat shows that the most common types of debt held by young Europeans (ages 18-34) are housing loans (31%), followed by student loans (22%), consumer credit (18%), and other loans (15%).

***Based On Average Amount of Debt:*** According to the same 2021 report by the Federal Reserve Bank of New York, the average student loan debt for young Americans is $22,200. The average credit card debt is $2,700, the average car loan debt is $18,400, and the average mortgage debt is $132,500.

A 2021 report by ING shows that the average debt of young Europeans (ages 18-34) is €22,100 (approximately $26,000), with significant differences across countries. For example, the average debt in Sweden is €7,700 (approximately $9,100), while in Greece it is €35,000 (approximately $41,000).

***Based On Overall Debt Levels:*** According to a 2021 report by the Federal Reserve Bank of New York, the total amount of household debt in the US was $14.6 trillion in the fourth quarter of 2020. Younger age groups (ages 18-29 and 30-39) held around 21% of that debt.

A 2019 report by Eurostat shows that the total amount of household debt in the European Union was €6.6 trillion (approximately $7.8 trillion) in 2018. Young Europeans (ages 18-34) held around 10% of that debt.

From the above statistics you would agree with me that **debt management** is a money skill that you must possess as a young individual. Circumstances might play out someday that may make you incur debt or you're probably in a debt as you're reading this book, hence why it's important that you take this seriously. But what exactly is *debt management?*

*Debt management refers to the process of taking steps to reduce and manage your debts effectively, usually with the goal of paying them off in a timely and responsible manner. This can involve creating a budget, prioritizing your debts, negotiating with creditors, and making timely payments to avoid late fees and penalties.*

As an example, let's say you are an adult who has accumulated several credit card debts over the years. Your monthly payments are starting to become overwhelming, and you're not sure how to get your finances under control. You decide to seek out a debt management plan to help you get back on track.

First, you work with a credit counseling agency to create a budget and determine how much you can realistically afford to pay towards your debts each month. Then, the agency negotiates with your creditors to lower your interest rates and monthly payments. With the reduced interest rates and a manageable payment plan, you're able to stay on top of your debts and make steady progress towards paying them off.

Over time, you continue to make consistent payments and slowly chip away at your debts. You also make adjustments to your budget as needed to ensure that you're not overspending and falling back into debt. Eventually, you reach the point where you've paid off all of your credit card debts, and you feel a sense of relief and accomplishment knowing that you've taken control of your finances and set yourself on a path towards financial stability.

## Understanding Different Types Of Debt

When it comes to managing debt, it's important to understand the different types of debt that exist. There are two main types of debt: *secured* and *unsecured*.

- **Secured Debt:** Secured debt is backed by collateral, which means that if you fail to make your payments, the lender can seize the collateral to recoup their losses. Examples of secured debt include mortgages and auto loans.

- **Unsecured Debt:** On the other hand, unsecured debt is not backed by collateral, which means that if you fail to make your payments, the lender has no specific asset to seize. Examples of unsecured debt include credit card debt and personal loans.

When I was younger, I didn't fully understand the differences between secured and unsecured debt. I ended up taking out a personal loan with a high interest rate, and it took me years to pay it off. Looking back, I wish I had taken the time to research my options and make a more informed decision. That's why it's important that as a young individual, you should know the basics of money, hence reading this book to the end.

It's also important to note that there are different types of interest rates associated with different types of debt. For example, credit cards often have higher interest rates than mortgages or auto loans, which can make them more difficult to pay off.

## Strategies For Paying Off Debt

In my years of research on personal finances and gaining financial stability, two effective strategies have stood out to me.

- The Debt Snowball Method: One effective strategy for paying off debt is the debt snowball method. This involves prioritizing your debts from smallest to largest and focusing on paying off the smallest debts first while making minimum payments on the others. Once you've paid off the smallest debt, you can then use the extra money to pay off the next smallest debt, and so on. This approach can help you build momentum and feel motivated as you see your debts disappear one by one.

Just like I hinted above, I had a lot of credit card debt and felt completely overwhelmed. But by focusing on paying off my smallest credit card balance first, I was able to gain momentum and motivation. Eventually, I was able to pay off all of my credit card debt using this method.

- **Debt Avalanche Method:** Another strategy is the debt avalanche method, which involves prioritizing your debts based on their interest rates. With this method, you focus on paying off the debt with the highest interest rate first, while making minimum payments on the others. Once you've paid off the highest interest rate debt, you can then use the extra money to pay off the next highest interest rate debt, and so on.

It's important to remember that there is no one-size-fits-all approach to paying off debt. You may need to try a few different strategies before finding one that works best for your individual situation.

## How To Avoid Getting into Debt in The First Place

Debt can be scary like I said at the beginning of the chapter. Sometimes, circumstances can be very unpredictable and hence smart and young individuals fall into debt. But then, there are some persons who because of their financial ineptitude created the problem for themselves. Let's examine how you can start avoiding getting into debt in the first place.

- Create a Budget: Creating a budget is not only helpful for paying off debt, but it's also an effective tool for avoiding debt in the first place. Make a list of all your income and expenses, and track your spending regularly to ensure that you're living within your means.

- Live Below Your Means: Avoid overspending and living beyond your means. Be mindful of your spending and stick to your budget, even when unexpected expenses arise.

- Avoid High-Interest Debt: Be cautious of high-interest debt, such as credit card debt. If you do use a credit card, pay off the balance in full each month to avoid interest charges.

- Save for Emergencies: Unexpected expenses, such as car repairs or medical bills, can quickly lead to debt if you're not prepared. Build an emergency fund to cover these types of expenses and avoid the need to borrow money.

- Avoid Impulse Purchases: Take time to consider your purchases before making them. Ask yourself if it's something you really need or if it's just a want. Avoid impulse purchases and stick to your budget.

- Prioritize Saving: Make saving a priority by setting aside a portion of your income each month for future goals. This can help you avoid the need to borrow money for large purchases, such as a car or a home.

Remember, the key to avoiding debt is to be mindful of your spending and to live within your means. By creating a budget, prioritizing saving, and avoiding high-interest debt, you can build a strong financial foundation and avoid the stress of debt.

# Chapter Four

## Saving And Investing

As a young man or woman who's just getting started with life, one of the best cultures you can imbibe is the culture of *saving and investing*. In conferences I have attended and called up to speak, I see young men and women asking some ridiculous questions about money. Just by their questions, it's not hard for me to know their kind of financial indiscipline. And one of them is *not having a savings and investing culture.*

I want you to be honest with yourself: *Do you have a savings and investment culture? Is saving and investing part of your lifestyle as a young man and woman?* If after looking inward for the answers you find yourself struggling to give account of how you save or invest money, you probably don't have a savings and investment culture.

Back to my story. I had the belief that once money came, it was meant to be spent. I was very erratic and undisciplined with money that came to my hands. I didn't even think about saving let alone investing because the idea of restraining yourself from spending a certain sum that was available seemed like a terrible punishment. And I know thousands of young Americans who struggle with saving and investing believe this too.

But is it really? Let's look at what savings and investing specifically means.

*Saving refers to the act of setting aside a portion of one's income or resources for future use, typically in a savings account, a money market account, or a certificate of deposit (CD).*

Savings are often used for short-term goals such as building an emergency fund or saving for a specific purchase like a vacation or a down payment on a house.

*Investing, on the other hand, refers to the act of putting money into an asset with the expectation of generating a return on that investment over time.*

Investments can include stocks, bonds, mutual funds, real estate, and other assets. Investing is typically used for long-term goals such as retirement or building wealth.

While both saving and investing involve setting aside money for the future, the key difference is that saving is typically focused on preserving the value of the money over time, while investing is focused on growing the value of the money over time. Both saving and investing can be important components of a healthy financial plan, and the specific mix of savings and investments will depend on an individual's financial goals, risk tolerance, and time horizon.

Next, why do you have to save? Let's find out.

## The Importance Of Saving For The Future

Saving money can be tough, especially when you're young, fabulous, and broke. But even if you're living paycheck to paycheck, it's important to start saving for the future. Why? Because you never know what life will throw your way.

For example, what if your car breaks down and you need to pay for expensive repairs? Or what if you lose your job and need to cover your expenses until you find a new one? Having a savings cushion can help you weather unexpected financial storms without having to rely on credit cards or loans.

But saving isn't just about preparing for emergencies. It's also about building a better future for yourself. By saving money now, you can:

- Save for a down payment on a house
- Pay for a wedding or other major life event
- Travel the world
- Start your own business
- Retire comfortably

Furthermore, savings can be of importance in the following ways:

- **Emergency fund:** Having savings set aside can provide a financial cushion in case of an unexpected event such as a job loss, a medical emergency, or a car repair. Having an emergency fund can help avoid the need to take on high-interest debt to cover these expenses.

- **Long-term goals**: Saving money can help achieve long-term financial goals such as buying a home, starting a business, or saving for retirement. By starting early and consistently saving, individuals can benefit from the power of compound interest and potentially grow their savings over time.

- **Financial security:** Having savings can provide a sense of financial security and reduce stress related to money management. Knowing that there is a financial buffer in place can help individuals feel more confident in their financial future.

- **Flexibility:** Having savings can provide flexibility and options in case of a job opportunity or a major life change. For example, having savings may allow an individual to take a lower-paying job that offers better long-term prospects, or take time off work to travel or pursue a passion.

Overall, saving money for the future can provide a sense of security, help achieve financial goals, and provide flexibility and options in case of unexpected events or opportunities. The bottom line? Saving money isn't always easy, but it's essential for your financial health and future.

## How To Start Saving, Even If You're Living Paycheck To Paycheck

Now that you know why saving is so important, let's talk about how to start saving, even if you're living paycheck to paycheck.

Here are the steps I followed when I started practicing having a savings' culture.

- **Budgeting:** The first step is to create a budget. Figure out how much money you have coming in each month, and then list all of your expenses. This will help you see where your money is going and identify areas where you can cut back. Budgeting is one of the basics from getting out of financial messes. Once you can discipline yourself to create a budget and stick to it, you are well on your way to financial freedom.

- **Automation:** Next, try to automate your savings. Many banks allow you to set up automatic transfers from your checking account to a savings account. You can also use apps like Digit or Qapital to automatically save small amounts of money each day. You can also look up other apps other than the above I mentioned. Just make sure it's something you can work with.

- **Go Extra:** Another way to save is to find ways to earn extra money. This could mean taking on a part-time job or freelancing on the side. Or, you could sell items you no longer need or use. Look around or within you. What is that one skill you possess you can use to fetch more money on the side? What is that one thing you possess as a property that can turn into a money-making machine for you?

Finally, try to stay motivated. Saving money can be hard, but it's worth it in the long run. Set goals for yourself and celebrate when you reach them. And remember, every little bit counts.

## Basic Investment Strategies for Young Beginners

Once you have some money saved up, you may want to consider investing it. Investing can help your money grow faster than it would in a savings account, but it's important to remember that investing always carries some degree of risk.

Here are some basic investment strategies for beginners:

- **Invest in a 401(k) or IRA**: If your employer offers a 401(k) plan, sign up and contribute as much as you can. If you don't have access to a 401(k), consider opening an individual retirement account (IRA). Both of these options allow you to invest your money in the stock market, which can help it grow over time.

- **Invest in Index Funds:** Index funds are a type of mutual fund that tracks a specific stock market index, like the S&P 500. They're a great option for beginners because they're low-cost and provide diversification.

- **Start small:** If you're new to investing, it's a good idea to start with a small amount of money. You can always increase your investments later on as you become more comfortable. From your savings, pull out something small and invest it just to get a thrill of what investment feels like.

- **Do Your Research**: Before investing in any company or fund, do your research. Look at its track record, read news articles, and talk to financial advisors if you have questions. Seek the opinion of those who have invested in a company or particular funding before you.

- **Stay diversified**: Don't put all of your eggs in one basket. Invest in a mix of stocks, bonds, and mutual funds. This way, you won't get burned when everything goes south as it may sometimes.

I'll be honest - investing has always intimidated me. I thought it was only for wealthy people who had extra money to throw around. But after talking to a financial advisor, I realized that investing can be a great way to grow your money over time.

I started by investing a small amount in a low-cost index fund, and I was surprised to see how quickly my money grew. It was exciting to see my money working for me, and it gave me the confidence to continue investing in other funds and stocks.

But, I learned that it's important to do your research before investing. I once invested in a company that I thought was a sure thing, but it ended up going bankrupt. It was a tough lesson, but it taught me to diversify my investments and never put all my eggs in one basket.

To wrap this up, savings and investing are yings and yangs that can turn the trajectory for your financial journey as a young individual for the better. Embrace it.

# Chapter Five

## Managing Your Money As A Young Individual

Managing your money as a young individual is a crucial skill that can have a significant impact on your financial well-being for years to come. Developing good money habits early on can help you build a solid foundation for achieving your financial goals, such as buying a house, starting a business, or retiring comfortably.

Here are some reasons why managing your money as a young individual is so important:

- You have time on your side: As a young individual, you have the advantage of time. By starting early, you can take advantage of the power of compounding interest, which means that the earlier you start saving and investing, the more time your money has to grow. This can help you reach your financial goals more quickly.

- You can avoid costly mistakes: By learning good money habits early on, you can avoid costly mistakes such as overspending, taking on too much debt, or failing to save for emergencies. These mistakes can have long-term consequences and can make it harder to achieve your financial goals.

- You can build good habits: Managing your money as a young individual can help you develop good habits that will serve you well throughout your life. By setting goals, creating a budget, and sticking to a savings plan, you can build the discipline and self-control needed to make wise financial decisions.

- You can reduce stress: Financial stress can take a toll on your mental and physical health. By managing your money well, you can reduce stress and anxiety and improve your overall well-being.

## Navigating The Challenges With Limited Financial Resources

If you're young and your income is pretty on the low side, here are some of the strategies you can use to navigate the challenges that come with it.

- **Prioritize Your Spending**: As a young adult with limited financial resources, it's important to prioritize your spending. Make a list of your needs and wants, and allocate your funds accordingly. For example, paying for rent, utilities, and groceries should take precedence over buying new clothes or eating out at expensive restaurants.

- **Track Your Expenses**: Keep track of your expenses using a budgeting app or spreadsheet. This will help you identify areas where you can cut back on spending and save more money.

- **Start Saving Early**: Even if you're only able to save a small amount each month, starting early can make a big difference in the long run. Consider setting up a savings account or investing in a low-risk investment fund.

- **Avoid Debt**: Credit card debt and other forms of high-interest debt can be a major financial burden for young adults. Try to avoid taking on too much debt, and pay off any existing debt as quickly as possible.

- **Look For Ways To Earn Extra Income:** Consider taking on a side hustle or part-time job to supplement your income. This can help you pay off debt faster, save more money, and build a solid financial foundation for your future.

## Tips For Managing Money in Your 20s and 30s

Your 20s and 30s are the period where you should already have a firm grasp of how you can manage your money.

I have put together some tips that can get you started.

- **Invest In Your Education:** One of the best investments you can make in your 20s and 30s is in your education. This can help you earn more money over the course of your career, and can also open up new opportunities for advancement.

- **Build An Emergency Fund:** Unexpected expenses can arise at any time, so it's important to have an emergency fund to fall back on. Aim to save at least 3-6 months' worth of living expenses in a separate savings account.

- **Set Financial Goals:** Setting financial goals can help you stay motivated and focused on your long-term financial objectives. Whether you're saving for a down payment on a house or planning for retirement, having clear goals in mind can help you make better financial decisions.

- **Invest For The Future:** As you start to build your wealth, consider investing in low-risk investment vehicles like index funds or ETFs. This can help your money grow over time and build a solid financial foundation for your future.

## Building a Solid Financial Foundation For Your Future.

- **Create A Long-term Financial Plan:** A long-term financial plan can help you stay on track and achieve your financial goals over time. Consider working with a financial planner or advisor to create a plan that fits your specific needs and goals.

- **Build A Diversified Investment Portfolio**: Diversifying your investments can help reduce risk and increase your chances of long-term success. Consider investing in a mix of stocks, bonds, and other assets to create a well-rounded portfolio.

- **Protect Yourself With Insurance**: Insurance can provide a safety net in case of unexpected events like illness, injury, or disability. Consider investing in health insurance, disability insurance, and life insurance to protect yourself and your family.

- **Stay Informed:** Keep up with financial news and trends to stay informed about changes in the market and opportunities for investment. This can help you make better decisions about your finances and stay ahead of the curve.

I hope these tips are helpful as you write your chapter on managing your money as a young adult. Remember, building a solid financial foundation takes time and effort, but the rewards are well

# Conclusion

As we conclude our journey through "Broke No More: A Money Blueprint for Young Ambition and Financial Resilience," it's clear that the path to financial empowerment is within your grasp. Throughout this book, we've explored a comprehensive range of topics aimed at equipping you with the tools to confidently manage your finances and pave the way to a secure financial future.

The foundation of our journey was laid with the understanding that financial literacy is not just an option, but a necessity in today's complex world. By delving into the intricacies of budgeting, debt management, saving, investing, and wise money practices as a young adult, we've aimed to provide you with a solid framework for navigating your financial landscape.

The significance of a positive money mindset was a recurring theme, reminding us that the way we approach money shapes our financial outcomes. By embracing abundance and veering away from scarcity, you're better prepared to overcome challenges and achieve your financial aspirations.

As you close this book, remember that knowledge is only as valuable as the actions you take. To put the lessons learned into practice, consider these actionable steps:

1. Create Your Financial Roadmap: Take the time to craft a detailed financial plan, incorporating budgeting techniques and strategies to pay off debt. Tailor it to your unique circumstances and goals.

2.     Start Saving Today: Regardless of your current financial situation, begin saving for the future. Even small contributions can accumulate over time and provide a safety net.

3.     Explore Investment Opportunities: Begin exploring basic investment strategies to grow your wealth. Start with cautious steps that match your risk tolerance and gradually expand your knowledge.

4.     Cultivate a Positive Money Mindset: Continuously work on cultivating a mindset of abundance and gratitude. This shift can transform the way you approach financial challenges and opportunities.

5.     Stay Educated: Keep learning about personal finance. Whether through books, online resources, or financial workshops, ongoing education will empower you to make informed decisions.

Your financial journey is ongoing, and with the principles outlined in this book, you have a roadmap to guide you toward a prosperous and secure future. Remember, you have the ability to break free from financial constraints and build a life of financial resilience and abundance. Your journey begins now.